ILLUSTRATED BOOK OF WORLD WAR II

ILLUSTRATED

BOOK OF WORLD WAR II

The first record in full-colour photographs

Introductions and other text by Peter Simkins, Keeper of the Department of Exhibits, Imperial War Museum

Published by Sidgwick & Jackson

INTRODUCTION

First published in Great Britain in 1972
by Sidgwick & Jackson Limited
Copyright © The Conway Picture Library and
Sidgwick & Jackson Limited
ISBN 0 283 97885 6
Printed in Great Britain by
Sir Joseph Causton and Sons Ltd., London and Eastleigh
for Sidgwick & Jackson Limited
1 Tavistock Chambers, Bloomsbury Way
London WC1A 2SG

The photographs in this book present a unique record in colour of one of the most critical periods in Britain's history. They form part of a much larger collection built up by the staff and photographers of *Illustrated*, one of Britain's leading pictorial news magazines of the time and, alas, now defunct. Most of the photographs were taken by *Illustrated*'s own staff photographers, while others, including the fascinating pictures of Hitler and Mussolini, were discovered and acquired by the magazine's reporters in Germany after the war.

They represent the best and most interesting pictures in the collection and many of them are being published for the first time, as censorship and wartime printing economies kept them out of the pages of *Illustrated* during the war years. This is the first book about the Second World War in which the photographs are entirely in colour and, as such, it adds a new dimension to the pictorial record of that conflict.

It is not the intention of this book to tell the complete story of the war but rather to reflect the nature and atmosphere of those years by highlighting various aspects of the struggle. History is nothing if it is not a study of people and individuals; from national, political and military leaders to ordinary men and women in and behind the lines, these are well-represented. Also depicted here are some of the significant weapons which helped to shape the course of the war. The global scale of the conflict is mirrored by the range of locations where these photographs were taken. We see pictures of Iceland and the Atlantic on the one hand and of India and Burma on the other. However, this is essentially a book about the British war effort and the majority of the photographs relate to Britain's fighting services and the men and women who led them or backed them up.

Photographers have been adding to the records of war for over a century. Fenton's pictures of the Crimean War and Brady's coverage of the American Civil War are already legendary. Thereafter, most armed conflicts were captured in one way or another by the camera until the First World War saw the detailed recording of events by artists, photographers and, for the first time on any scale, the cine-cameraman, adopted as a deliberate official policy by the governments of most of the belligerent nations.

During the First World War, photography was to prove of immense value to the armies. With the deadlock of trench warfare, the cavalry were unable to carry out their traditional reconnaissance duties and the aerial camera became an essential piece of equipment to the army staffs wishing to see 'the other side of the hill' and to build up a detailed picture of enemy troop movements and concentrations, the location of supply dumps, and the extent to which their own attacks or artillery bombardments had been successful.

The 1914-1918 conflict also saw photography mobilized for propaganda purposes. The British public of 1916 could find plenty of photographs of smiling British 'Tommies' wearing captured German helmets, but few pictures of the dead heaped in front of the German barbed wire on the Somme front. The 35-millimetre camera enabled the photographers of the Second World War to present a much more accurate picture of that conflict and to leave a pictorial record of unprecedented size and scope. Most governments had by now learned how to make the maximum use of the mass media, but propaganda, and with it censorship, was much more subtle. Cameramen were allowed right into the front lines and the records of the Second World War are full of outstanding action photographs. The growth of radio, film newsreels and the mass circulation newspapers and magazines had created a tremendous appetite for news of all kinds, particularly during wartime, to which governments and the press were forced to respond. Official control over the news was at least partly achieved by mobilizing the reporters and photographers themselves. Most of the branches of the armed forces of nations on both sides had their own photographers and, in Britain, many newspapers and magazines lost 75 per cent of their staff photographers. A considerable number became official photographers.

This tended to limit further what was published at home for only official photographers were allowed to work in overseas theatres, inevitably leading to a certain similarity in many of the pictures appearing in the British press during the war. Censorship for the newspaper and magazine editors came partly from above and was partly self-imposed. Anything which contained information which might be useful to the enemy was inevitably prohibited, but censorship often derived from advice rather than coercion.

If newspapers wished to cover a story where security might be involved, the copy could be submitted to the Scrutiny Division of the Ministry of Information. The censorship, however, remained to some extent voluntary. News items could be cut or banned, but they were rarely actually re-written by the government. Nevertheless, the freedom of the press, one of the principles for which Britain was fighting, was often more illusory than real.

These difficulties are naturally reflected in the pictures published here. *Illustrated* photographers could cover the personal interest stories for which there is such a great demand in the age of Everyman. People like to see themselves. On the other hand, the cameramen of the newspapers and magazines were not encouraged to photograph such things as radar installations or the interiors of aircraft, tanks and warships. Bonny wartime babies were one thing; the layout of the cockpit of a Mosquito was quite another. However, if the image of the war presented here is a little artificial, a little stylized and a little cosy, this is just as revealing of the policy and mood of the age as the front-line action photograph.

In describing the photographs here, several problems were encountered. Many of the pictures were well-documented and recorded in the files and record sheets compiled by the photographers and staff of *Illustrated*. Others, unfortunately, were not, again for reasons of censorship or because, as in the case of the Hitler photographs, all records had disappeared. As much information as is available has generally been given. To some extent this involved a great deal of detective work. For instance, in the case of the photograph of the Sunderland flying boat, it was possible to discover where the picture was taken by looking at the Squadron code letters on the fuselage of the aircraft. Once these had been deciphered, and knowing from the *Illustrated* files when the picture was taken, it was a fairly easy matter to look up the records of the squadrons of Coastal Command to find out where that particular squadron had been stationed at that time. Details of dress and uniform, the design of weapons and pieces of equipment, camouflage schemes and known facts about the careers of various personalities—all helped to gather information about other photographs if only by a process of elimination. In some of the photographs, the process of elimination and deduction can only take you to within approximate limits. Wherever it has been impossible to establish the precise background of a picture, the caption remains deliberately vague. This is to avoid misleading the reader, but, in such cases, it was felt that the interest of the picture was still sufficient to warrant its inclusion. Indeed, if readers can help to fill some of the gaps, the author and publishers would welcome it.

This detective work was considerably eased by the magnificent reference collections of the Imperial War Museum and the knowledge and expertise of my colleagues. However, a great debt is owed to the many non-professional students of war, whose numbers are increasing each day and who now fill the ranks of the model soldier, war games and aircraft preservation societies which are springing up all over Britain. Interest in military history has never been so wide and many of these people have contributed much to our knowledge of the subject by delving into minute aspects of the two World Wars and shedding light in corners into which the professional historians have, by reason of their limited numbers, been unable to peer. Such enthusiasts enable us to put flesh on the skeleton of our knowledge of history.

1 LEADERS

The success or failure of the leaders portrayed in the following pages depended, to a considerable extent, on the degree to which they were able to project the national will in their own person. It is, of course, debatable whether the peoples of the belligerent powers were initially conscious of what their will actually was. Some, like Hitler and Mussolini, had been able to shape the national will to their own beliefs and ambitions, partly by being able to exploit the dissatisfaction of their compatriots with the existing political and economic situation in the 1920s and 1930s, and partly by the sheer force of their own personalities. Others, like Churchill and de Gaulle, emerged from a relative wilderness at a time when their peoples had come close to, or had actually known, defeat. The leaders of Britain and France during the inter-war years, now the scapegoats for the disasters of 1940, had, in fact, done no more than reflect the general desire of their nations never to undergo another experience such as they had suffered between 1914 and 1918. When the full extent of the Nazi menace was realized, the national will changed and with it the leaders. Finally, other men became national leaders some years after the war. Eden and Eisenhower, both popular and able subordinates during the war years, took the centre of the political stage in their respective countries in the 1950s, at least partly on the strength of their wartime achievements. De Gaulle, moreover, emerged a second time from the wilderness, again at a time of national crisis.

Yet, for whatever reasons these leaders had come to power, the extent to which they were able to retain and exercise power also depended on the popular image they were able to present. Their leadership may originally have stemmed from popular support; once in power they were able to manipulate that support, with varying degrees of success.

In the age of mass circulation newspapers and magazines, cinema newsreels and radio broadcasts, the means of manipulating popular support were more extensive in scope than at any time previously. The different techniques used by the various leaders portrayed here are interesting in themselves. Hitler and Mussolini both realized, at an early stage in their careers, the overwhelming importance of the new mass media to them in their struggle to achieve power and retain it. Vast parades and rallies, colourful uniforms and banners, torchlight processions and bands – all undoubtedly had an appeal at a time of widespread economic depression and diverted attention from the less desirable aspects of the Nazi and Fascist ideologies. Even the arts were utilized to project the images of the new regimes. Leni Riefenstahl's film *The Triumph of the Will* still retains a feeling of tremendous purpose and power and one can see how easy it must have been to let oneself be seduced by the theatrical trappings of the Nazi regime. The graphic arts and architecture also reflected these techniques. Yet it is often forgotten that Hitler's image in Germany was built up almost entirely in the years before the Second World War. After 1940, his public appearances and speeches became less and less frequent as he became more and more involved in the purely military aspects of the war. The fact that he could retain popular support was as much a tribute to the strength of the Nazi propaganda machine as to the fear which the regime could also arouse. By 1943 it was Goebbels, more than anybody, who put the words into the mouths of Germans and made them think that it was their own will that was being voiced. Few examples of mass hypnosis, even in the Nazi era, match Goebbels' 'Do you want total war?' speech in 1943. For all the Italian love of the theatrical, Mussolini was never quite able to master propaganda techniques to the same extent and this may help to explain why his support disappeared so rapidly in the face of Allied invasion whereas some Nazis continued to fight until the very heart of Berlin fell to the Russians.

Churchill too, in a typically British way, was able to embody the national will in his own person. A master of the English language, he succeeded, in his wartime speeches, in saying what the British people wished they could have said for themselves. Traditionally suspicious of demagogues, the British were nevertheless able to identify themselves with their Prime Minister who was clearly above them but somehow uniquely theirs. If they would not have accepted circuses, they could accept the understated personal symbols such as Churchill's cigar and 'V-sign' and Montgomery's black beret. De Gaulle's appeal lay in his aloof and incorruptible image which contrasted sharply with the generation of French politicians who had led France to the humiliation of 1940. While he, too, symbolized a nation's determination, he achieved his popular support almost without any direct contact with the mass of the French people. Almost unknown outside military circles before 1940, and never a brilliant orator, de Gaulle was able to lead the French to a recovery of national pride in 1944 because of his very remoteness. He was the only national figure who was seen to be completely untainted by the shame of defeat. Few men can have come to national prominence with as little help from the mass media in their own country.

Whatever the qualities or faults of the men portrayed here, their successors, with notable exceptions, have generally come to be regarded as men of lesser stature. Distance may lend enchantment to the view, for, apart from Eden (now Lord Avon), all are dead. What may be said with certainty, however, is that few of today's leaders have been able to symbolize the national will to the same extent as the leaders of the Second World War.

Previous page: A meeting between the German and Italian dictators during the Second World War. There are no records with the *Illustrated* photographic files to confirm when this particular meeting between Hitler and Mussolini actually took place. The fact that Hitler is wearing field grey, which he symbolically adopted on the outbreak of war, suggests that it is certainly a post-1939 photograph, and it was undoubtedly taken before Mussolini's fall from power in 1943. The fact that both leaders are wearing greatcoats suggests that it was an autumn or winter meeting. The most likely solution is that it was taken on 28 October 1940, the day Italian forces invaded Greece across the Albanian frontier. Hitler came straight from a meeting with Marshal Pétain at Montoire to see Mussolini in Florence and to try to advise him not to invade Greece because of the dangers of a Balkan uproar. Two hours before the Führer reached Florence he was told that Italian troops had already crossed the frontier. In the event Hitler reacted with restraint and promised support for Italy. The fact that the train is obviously German and the officers in the receiving line are Italian support the suggestion that the photograph was taken at this meeting. At another winter meeting, at Pusch station in January 1941, the Führer, according to Ciano, was wearing a leather greatcoat.

Overleaf: Winston Churchill (later Sir Winston), at his desk in March 1944 (the picture was not published by *Illustrated* until after V-E Day). Although taken when victory was in sight, the photograph expresses all the bulldog defiance that kept the country together in 1940. He is holding the inevitable cigar, which became, with his famous 'V' for Victory sign, almost his personal symbol during the war years. Churchill was Prime Minister from May 1940 until the General Election in 1945, and again from October 1951 until April 1955. His power and popularity during the Second World War, when he seemed by his speeches and actions to embody the will of the British people, is by now legendary. Public opinion polls between July 1940 and May 1945 show that never less than 78 per cent of those interviewed said they approved of Churchill's Premiership, and never more than 6 per cent said they disapproved. Yet, as the dangers of 1940 receded, the Churchillian magic undoubtedly dwindled. In fact, as the war progressed, he led an increasingly disunited nation to a chorus of personal attacks. Aneurin Bevan once said of him 'that he fights debates like a war and the war like a debate'. Whatever the public felt about Churchill as a war leader and statesman, their rejection of him in the 1945 election showed that their opinion of him as a peacetime politician was rather different.

General Dwight D. Eisenhower talks to an American
soldier during pre-invasion manoeuvres in England,
February 1944. Air Chief Marshal Sir Arthur Tedder
(left) and General Sir Bernard Montgomery (centre)
look on. Eisenhower (as Supreme Commander),
Tedder (as Deputy Supreme Commander) and
Montgomery (as commander of 21st Army Group)
were perhaps the three key figures in the planning
and execution of Operation Overlord, the Allied
invasion of Normandy in June 1944. By the time this
picture was taken there were well over 1,000,000
American servicemen and women in Great Britain.

all Frenchmen to join with me in continuing the fight . . . Whatever happens, the flame of French resistance must not, and will not, be extinguished.' As leader, and eventually President of the French Committee of National Liberation in Algiers, he became the symbol of French resistance and a firm ally of the Western powers. In September 1944, with the liberation of France, he formed a provisional government, resigning as Prime Minister in 1946 and forming the R.P.F. Party *(Rassemblement du Peuple Français)* which expressed popular discontent with weak parliamentary governments and exploited anti-Communist feelings. By 1953 the party had disbanded and de Gaulle lapsed into relative obscurity until the Algerian Crisis of 1958, threatening France with civil war, brought him back to power as the only man likely to save the situation. He was President of the Fifth Republic from December 1958 until his resignation in 1969. He died the following year, in 1970.

Anthony Eden, with his dog 'Nipper', at his country home near Chichester, March 1945. The elegance and charm which so captivated the House of Commons can be discerned in this informal study. Eden was Secretary of State for Foreign Affairs from 1935 until 1938, when he resigned after a disagreement with Chamberlain. He subsequently held the posts of Secretary of State for Dominion Affairs (1939–40), for War (1940), and finally became Foreign Secretary again, in Churchill's government, from 1940 until 1945. Foreign Secretary and Deputy Prime Minister in the Conservative government from 1951 to 1955, he finally succeeded to the Premiership in April 1955 and held office during the Suez Crisis in 1956. He resigned in January 1957.

General Charles de Gaulle, photographed at the Free French Headquarters in London on 16 February 1943. He was then in his early fifties, and displaying the intransigence and sense of destiny which became even more apparent in his later career. Churchill was frequently exasperated by de Gaulle's arrogance—at the same time the General usually got his way. In May 1940 he had been appointed Brigadier-General in command of the newly-formed French 4th Armoured Division which fought effectively in the disastrous campaign which followed the German *blitzkreig* in France. On 6 June, Reynaud appointed him Under-secretary of State for War, his first political appointment, which took him twice to London and meetings with Churchill. When Pétain asked for an armistice, de Gaulle returned to London, putting himself at the head of the Free French movement. On 18 June he broadcast his famous appeal: 'France has lost a battle, but France has not lost the war . . . I invite

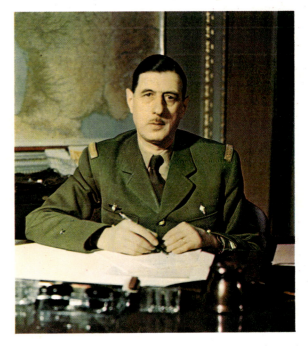

These photographs of Mussolini were probably
taken in August 1941, when he visited
Hitler's headquarters on the Eastern Front,
following the German attack on Russia. Other
photographs in the *Illustrated* collection, showing
Mussolini reviewing Italian troops in the company
of German officers and obviously taken on the same
occasion, support this view. Although Mussolini's
offer of Italian troops for the Eastern Front was not
welcomed in Berlin, he was determined to send them
and eventually a force of 200,000 Italian soldiers was
sent. Mussolini became irritated at the over-
emphasis on German successes by the German news
releases and was secretly pleased whenever the
Germans ran into resistance, saying that he hoped
that '. . . in the East the Germans will lose a lot of
feathers'. During this tour of the Russian front he
was also obviously annoyed when General Messe's
Turin Division, already with the German armies in
Russia, looked clean and well-shaved, instead of
appearing like battle-scarred veterans in front of
Hitler. He also complained that Hitler left him
talking to von Rundstedt when the Führer went up
to talk to some German troops. 'Did you notice how
unsoldierly the Führer looked?' he later asked
Alfieri, his Press Minister.

Hitler (left foreground) talks to other Nazi leaders, possibly at his headquarters on the Eastern Front in 1941 or 1942. Hitler's field grey uniform confirms that this is a wartime photograph. Also in the picture are von Ribbentrop (centre) and Goering (right). Behind von Ribbentrop and between him and Goering is Himmler. The naval officer partly obscured by Hitler is probably Grand-Admiral Raeder.

Right: Hitler addressing a German army gathering, possibly at Potsdam. The photograph was probably taken before the Second World War. Although there is little evidence to confirm where and when it was taken, it clearly indicates the theatrical nature of Nazi ceremonial.

Hitler reviewing detachments, possibly of the S.A., at a Party Day Rally in Nuremberg. The shape of the helmet worn by the S.S. man on the left suggests that the picture was taken in 1935 or after. The S.S. man is in fact holding the Blood Flag of the Nazi Party. Note the S.A. band in the background, indicating that S.A. detachments were being reviewed as the photograph was taken.

A diplomatic reception in Berlin before the Second World War. In the foreground von Ribbentrop, the German Foreign Minister, is talking to Cardinal Cesare Orsenigo, Papal Nuncio and doyen of the diplomatic corps in Germany. Behind them, Hitler is talking to another diplomat. The form of diplomatic dress worn by von Ribbentrop and the Chief of Protocol (behind Hitler) suggests that the picture was taken in 1939, but before September, as Hitler began to wear field grey with the advent of war. It may well show the New Year reception of that year when, as in previous years, the foreign ambassadors came to pay their respects to the head of the German state. Heinrich Hoffmann, Hitler's photographer, later wrote: '. . . never in my life have I ever photographed so much fervent friendship and hand-shaking as at these New Year receptions.'

A study of Hitler in a relaxed mood before the
Second World War, as he takes a boat trip, possibly
on the Tegernsee in Bavaria, or on the Königsee
near Berchtesgaden. Intriguingly, the girl in the
photograph bears a strong resemblance to his niece
and, according to some sources, his 'one great love',
Geli Raubal, for whom Hitler had a strong
infatuation or even affection between 1929 and 1931.
As Geli Raubal committed suicide in 1931 this
seems unlikely, for colour photographs of Hitler are
extremely rare before 1933–34. However, her
proximity to Hitler in this photograph suggests that
it might well in fact be her.

Hitler, in civilian clothes, in the 1930s. The style of
the little girl's costume suggests that the picture was
taken in Bavaria. The man behind Hitler and the
young girl in the centre of the picture appears to be
Heinrich Hoffmann, Hitler's photographer, thus
suggesting that the picture may have been taken by
Hugo Jaeger. Certainly, Hoffmann, one of Hitler's
intimates, would have been allowed to be this close
to the Führer by his bodyguards. Hitler, who saw in
them the future of the 'Thousand-Year Reich', was
constantly photographed with children and members
of Nazi youth organizations.

2 WEAPONS AND WARFARE

The nature of warfare has changed more since the Crimean War than in any comparable period since the introduction of gunpowder. The history of warfare may, in one sense, be described in terms of the continual see-saw of weapon development. Ever since man developed the shield and armour to meet the threat of the spear, arrow, and club, the conduct of war has been determined by the relative superiority, at any one time, of defensive or offensive weapons. By the Second World War the balance had swung once more, this time in favour of the offensive. The tank, the submarine and the aeroplane had all been used, with varying degrees of success, in the 1914-1918 conflict. Indeed, the unrestricted U-boat warfare of 1917 had brought Britain close to defeat. The same year, unopposed daylight attacks on London by German bombing aircraft led directly to the creation of the Royal Air Force as an independent Service in 1918 with the doctrine of strategic bombing as its 'raison d'être'. With the first tentative take-offs of aircraft from warships during these years, the aircraft carrier and a new role for naval air power had also begun to emerge. At the outbreak of war in 1939, all these weapons or weapons systems had reached a stage of development which ensured the restoration of mobility to warfare and transformed the nature of the conflict. But it is not just a question of what the weapons are; it is also a question of how they are used. Parity in weapons is not enough if doctrine is based on false assumptions, if leadership is indecisive or inflexible, or if morale is poor. This fact can be illustrated by the Battle of France in 1940. The 'blitzkrieg' (or lightning war) strategy and tactics employed by the Germans in May and June of that year can be traced back to the ideas of outstanding British military thinkers during the inter-war years, particularly Captain Basil Liddell Hart and Major-General J. F. C. Fuller. Yet these men were largely prophets without honour in their own country. Thus while the British and French High Commands stumbled into the age of mechanized warfare, which they themselves had done much to create, it was the Germans who first realized the full potential of the new ideas. The French and British armies in 1940 had at least as many tanks as the Germans. Although these tanks had a more limited range than those of the enemy, the French had armoured fighting vehicles of greater toughness and hitting-power. It was in organization and doctrine that the Allies were inferior. The French, and to some extent the British, were bound by a Maginot Line mentality. The French used their armour partly as mechanized cavalry and partly as a means of supporting their infantry, so the tempo of the advance was restricted to the speed with which the infantry and artillery could be brought forward. The Germans, on the other hand, by grouping their mechanized forces in armoured divisions and corps, were able to concentrate large numbers of tanks at the decisive points and make deep thrusts into and beyond the Franco-British front. Having developed, to a high degree, the technique of co-operation between armoured columns and dive-bombers, the pace of the German advance was dictated by the tanks and not by the infantry. The success of the German onslaught in France in 1940 is a good illustration of the fact that weapons do not win battles by themselves.

The photographs in this section illustrate some of the more interesting trends in weapon development by the middle years of the Second World War. The Lancaster and the Mosquito, two of the most significant aircraft of the war, are both represented. The Avro Lancaster was perhaps the most famous and certainly the most successful heavy bomber of the war. Even though the Royal Air Force had been created with the concept of strategic bombing at the very heart of its doctrine it had entered the war in 1939 without the equipment or the techniques to perform such a role successfully. The Lancaster, which first came into operational use in March 1942, became the mainstay of Bomber Command by the end of the war and, more than any other bombing aircraft, enabled the Royal Air Force to perform the strategic role for which it had initially been designed. By March 1945 there were over fifty squadrons of Lancasters in operational service with Bomber Command. Capable of carrying up to 22,000 lbs. of bombs, and having taken part in some of the most famous operations of the war, including the Dams Raid of 1943, Lancasters flew more than 156,000 sorties and had dropped over 608,000 tons of bombs by the end of the conflict. The De Havilland Mosquito, with its revolutionary wooden construction, was undoubtedly the most versatile aircraft of the war. With a speed of nearly 400 m.p.h., it could carry up to 4,000 lbs. of bombs, and was equally successful as a low-level bomber, a pathfinder aircraft for the main bombing force, a high-speed intruder bomber, a night fighter, a rocket-firing tactical fighter-bomber, an anti-shipping strike aircraft with Coastal Command or as a photographic reconnaissance machine. Together with the Spitfire, here represented by its naval version, the Seafire, these machines were the most outstanding products of the British aircraft industry in the 1930s and early 1940s.

Special weapons were also developed for more specialized tasks. The Crocodile flame-thrower tank was one of these and represents the range of tanks known as 'funnies' which helped to breach the Atlantic Wall and establish the beachhead in Normandy in 1944. These specialized armoured vehicles included bridge-laying tanks, swimming or amphibious tanks to go ashore in the assault waves and flail tanks fitted with chains on a revolving drum to explode any mines which might lie in front of the vehicle.

The 'forgotten' campaign in Burma is recalled to mind by the pictures of the struggle for Fort Dufferin, Mandalay, in March 1945. In many respects, the story of the campaign in Burma is symbolic of the whole conduct of the war by the Allies, in that initial reverses were followed by a slow recovery and then decisive victory. It can also be regarded as a microcosm of the Allied effort in that a multi-national force, commanded by a sailor, Admiral Lord Louis Mountbatten, and supplied and supported by air power, won a major victory on land in the successful advances of 1944 and 1945. Finally, the picture of H.M.S. *Indomitable* serves to remind us of the decisive influence which air power exerted on naval operations during the Second World War. The emergence of the aircraft carrier did more than anything else to consign the big-gun battleship to the scrapyard. The Battle of the Coral Sea in May 1942 and the Battle of Midway, the following month, were fought entirely by carrier-borne aircraft, without the opposing fleets ever coming into surface contact with each other. Even in the action in the Surigao Strait, during the Battle of Leyte Gulf in October 1944, which proved to be the last surface action fought between battleships, most enemy losses were inflicted by air attack. But, less than a year later, Hiroshima and Nagasaki ushered in a new and even more frightening stage in weapon development.

Previous pages (left): A Crocodile, or Churchill flame-thrower tank, in action during a petroleum warfare demonstration in October 1944. The development of this weapon had begun in 1941, the design being finalized and put into production in 1943. The Churchill VII tank became the standard Crocodile vehicle and enough were ready by D-Day to contribute significantly to the success of the Normandy landings and the breaching of the German 'Atlantic Wall'. Crocodiles saw service throughout the campaign in north-west Europe and were also used in Italy.

Previous pages (right): The crew of Lancaster ZN–Y: W4118 of No. 106 Squadron, R.A.F. Bomber Command, nicknamed 'Admiral Prune', watch as their aircraft is loaded-up for a mine-laying operation on 9 November 1942. A Manchester bomber of the same squadron can be seen in the background. The squadron had been operating from Coningsby but had moved to Syerston, where this picture was taken, in October 1942 when runways were being laid at their own station. The squadron was then commanded by Wing Commander Guy Gibson who, the following May, won the Victoria Cross when he led No. 617 Squadron in the famous low-level precision attack on the Möhne and Eder Dams. The Lancaster bomber featured in this picture was lost on 5 February 1943.

Another photograph of the Crocodile flame-thrower tank demonstrating its capabilities in October 1944. Its equipment included an armoured two-wheeled trailer containing some 400 gallons of fuel. With the help of five pressure bottles containing nitrogen, pressurized fuel passed from the trailer to the flame projector in the tank's hull through a device known as the 'Link'. The average range of the projected flame was 80 yards, although 120 yards was possible under favourable conditions, and the projector could fire 80 one-second bursts or a continuous spout of flame. A quick-release device could be used to jettison the trailer, if damaged. The flame projector replaced the hull machine-gun of the Churchill VII which retained its 75 mm. main armament and could still be used as a normal gun tank.

A Wasp flame-thrower vehicle goes through its paces at a petroleum warfare demonstration in October 1944. The Wasp was a modified Universal Carrier, developed by the Petroleum Warfare Department between 1941 and 42. It was fitted with two flame-fuel tanks, carrying 100 gallons in all. Pressure bottles and other equipment were all stowed inside the Carrier. The flame projector had a range of 80–100 yards. The vehicle was otherwise unarmed and carried a crew of two. This model appears to be the Mark II version, introduced in 1943, which had a flame projector mounted in the machine-gun housing of the Carrier, making the vehicle less recognizable as a flame-thrower. Wasp Mark IIs were used by 21st Army Group in Europe in 1944–45. The Carrier was not, in fact, a Bren Gun Carrier; the latter was a modified carrier, developed in 1938, to take a Bren Gun. To avoid proliferation of versions of the basic machine, the Universal Carrier was produced in 1940 for all purposes and became the standard combat carrier during the war, although the name Bren Gun Carrier stuck and was widely, but erroneously, used throughout the period.

Previous page: Observers look down from Pagoda Hill on the battle raging below for the possession of Fort Dufferin in March 1945. A fortress of immense strength, Fort Dufferin had been built by King Mindon when he established his capital at Mandalay in 1858, and was renamed after the Earl of Dufferin, the Viceroy of India when northern Burma was annexed by Britain in 1886. Its walls, 23 ft high, were 30 ft thick at the base and some 12 ft thick at the top. The fort was surrounded by a moat, 40 ft wide and bridged in five places, and massive buttresses defiladed the angled gates in each wall. The remnants of the Japanese 60th Regiment defended the fort.

Left: Indian machine-gunners on Pagoda Hill during the battle for Fort Dufferin, Mandalay. The task of capturing the fort was entrusted to Lieutenant-General Sir Montague Stopford's XXXIII Corps. The 19th Indian Division began the assault on the night of 8–9 March 1945, but despite repeated infantry attacks, supported by low-level air attacks and almost point-blank bombardments by medium artillery, the Japanese defenders still held out on 19 March.

Below: The Union Jack is raised in Fort Dufferin, Mandalay, following its capture by the 19th Indian Division on 20 March 1945. Between 17 and 19 March, air and artillery attacks had opened a number of breaches in the north and east walls, and, just after midday on the 20th, following a heavy air attack, six Burmese emerged to report that there were no Japanese left in the fort. Men of the 62nd Indian Infantry Brigade and a medium artillery regiment secured the fort by 1.30 p.m.

General Sir Frederick Pile, Commander-in-Chief of
Anti-Aircraft Command from 1939 to 1945, is
pictured here with the crew of a quick-firing 40 mm.
Bofors light anti-aircraft gun in December 1942.
The Bofors Gun, developed before the war by the
Bofors Company in Sweden, was a simple, robust
and formidable weapon which could fire some 120
impact-fused rounds per minute. Produced in
quantity in Britain from 1941, it was, in its various
forms, one of the most widely-used weapons of the
war. It was particularly effective against low-flying
aircraft because of its rapid elevation and traverse
and its quick-firing characteristics.

3·7-inch anti-aircraft guns firing at night in
December 1942. One of the best anti-aircraft weapons
of the Second World War, it was just beginning to
be produced in small numbers as war came. It
subsequently became one of the mainstays of Anti-
Aircraft Command. Originally loaded by manpower,
it was equipped during the war with the Molins
fuse-setter and loader-rammer device. By making
the fuse-setting, loading and ramming part of a
mechanical sequence, this device helped to double
the rate of fire and increased accuracy by removing
some of the variable factors in the process.

A convoy passes through the Straits of Dover in
October 1944. While the Germans had occupied the
Channel coast of France, Allied shipping passing
through the Straits had been prey to attacks from the
Luftwaffe, from E-boats, and from German coastal
artillery, combining to make this one of the most
dangerous stretches of water in the world. By
October 1944, as the war moved towards the
German frontiers, the Straits were relatively
peaceful, although the escorting warships in this
picture are still laying a precautionary smokescreen.

The depth charge crew of a trawler of the Royal
Naval Patrol Service at the ready in E-boat Alley
in March 1943. E-boat Alley was the name given
to the North Sea by convoy skippers, especially to
the section between the Thames and the Tweed,
because of the dangers of attack from the fast
German E-boats or submarines. The requisitioned
and converted trawlers and drifters of the R.N.P.S.
helped to defend the coastal convoys and to remove
the dangers. They kept ports open, swept channels
for the merchantmen, and acted as anti-submarine
vessels. These small craft, sometimes referred to
as the 'Lilliput Fleet' became an important arm in
the war at sea.

Below: A 21-inch torpedo is hoisted from the submarine depot ship H.M.S. *Forth*, to be stowed in a submarine lying alongside. Experience in the First World War had shown the need for depot ships to provide repair facilities and base services for smaller flotilla craft. The *Forth*, built specially for the purpose, was launched at Clydebank in 1938, and was serving with the 3rd Submarine Flotilla when this photograph was taken in June 1943.

Opposite above: Submarines of the 3rd Submarine Flotilla alongside the depot ship H.M.S. *Forth*, probably at Holy Loch, in June 1943. The *Forth*'s sister ship, H.M.S. *Maidstone*, was used in 1971 to house internees in Northern Ireland.

Opposite below: Another view of submarines alongside H.M.S. *Forth*, June 1943. The one on the right is the former German submarine U-570. This type of VIIc U-boat, launched in 1941, had been depth-charged and forced to surrender by the crew of a Hudson aircraft of No. 269 Squadron, Royal Air Force, 80 miles south of Iceland on 27 August 1941. She subsequently became H.M.S. *Graph* and served with the Royal Navy in home waters until she was wrecked in March 1944.

Overleaf: Hellcats of the Fleet Air Arm on the flight deck of the aircraft carrier H.M.S. *Indomitable* in January 1945, during the attack on Japanese-held oil refineries in Sumatra. Aircraft carriers of the British Pacific Fleet had sailed from Ceylon in December 1944 to attack the refinery near Belawan Deli. On 24 January, a heavier blow was launched at Palembaung, where the two largest refineries in south-east Asia were located, capable of meeting two-thirds of Japanese requirements for aviation fuel. Forty-three Grumman Avengers, with fighter cover, took part in this attack, which, despite heavy opposition, damaged the Pladjoe refinery and halved its output at one stroke. Seven aircraft were lost (two to flak) although the Fleet Air Arm fighters accounted for fourteen Japanese aircraft. On 29 January, forty-six Avengers hit the refinery at Soengei Gerong, stopping production for two months. Even at the end of March, the two plants were only working at one-third of their capacity. Sixteen aircraft were lost in this latter strike, although Fleet Air Arm fighters had a successful day, destroying thirty in aerial combat and thirty-eight on the ground. The Grumman Hellcats in this picture were from either 1839 or 1844 Squadron, each of which had fourteen. These Hellcats formed part of the fighter escort.

Previous pages: Mosquitoes of R.A.F. Coastal Command take off at dawn on 4 December 1944 to strike at enemy shipping off the coast of Norway.

Left: Supermarine Seafire fighters of the Fleet Air Arm peel off for a practice attack during training in May 1943. The decision to adapt the famous Spitfire for carrier-borne service with the Fleet Air Arm had been taken in 1941, the Seafire IB being little more than a converted Spitfire VB. Later variants were specially produced for a naval air role, the Seafire III, the major Merlin-powered version, being fitted with folding wings for carrier service. Some 370 Seafire IICs and 1,200 IIICs were built during the war.

Below: Seafires of the Fleet Air Arm in line abreast, May 1943. Seafires first entered service in June 1942, and, by V–E Day, twelve first-line squadrons of the Fleet Air Arm were equipped with them, all but four with the Mk III version which was introduced to operations in 1943. Seafires saw action during the Allied landings in North Africa in November 1942, at Salerno in September 1943, and in Normandy and southern France in 1944, also serving in the Far East during 1945. Merlin-powered Seafires finally disappeared from service in 1946.

Overleaf: A Short Sunderland flying boat of No. 201 Squadron, R.A.F. Coastal Command, taking off from Lough Erne in Ireland in 1945 to patrol the lonely wastes of the Atlantic. It is camouflaged white for concealment among the clouds which are prevalent in northern latitudes. During the Second World War, Sunderlands patrolled ceaselessly over 5,000,000 miles of ocean in all weathers, and there was scarcely a moment when a Sunderland was not airborne somewhere in the Atlantic, the North Sea, the Mediterranean, the Indian Ocean, and the Pacific, hunting for U-boats, guarding convoys, and watching for the movements of enemy warships. They accounted for over thirty German submarines and with their 10–18 machine-guns, 250 lb. depth charges, and anti-submarine bombs, they were sufficiently heavily-armed to be called 'Flying Porcupines' by the Germans. The Sunderland had a normal duration of $13\frac{1}{2}$ hours and a maximum range of 2,880 miles.

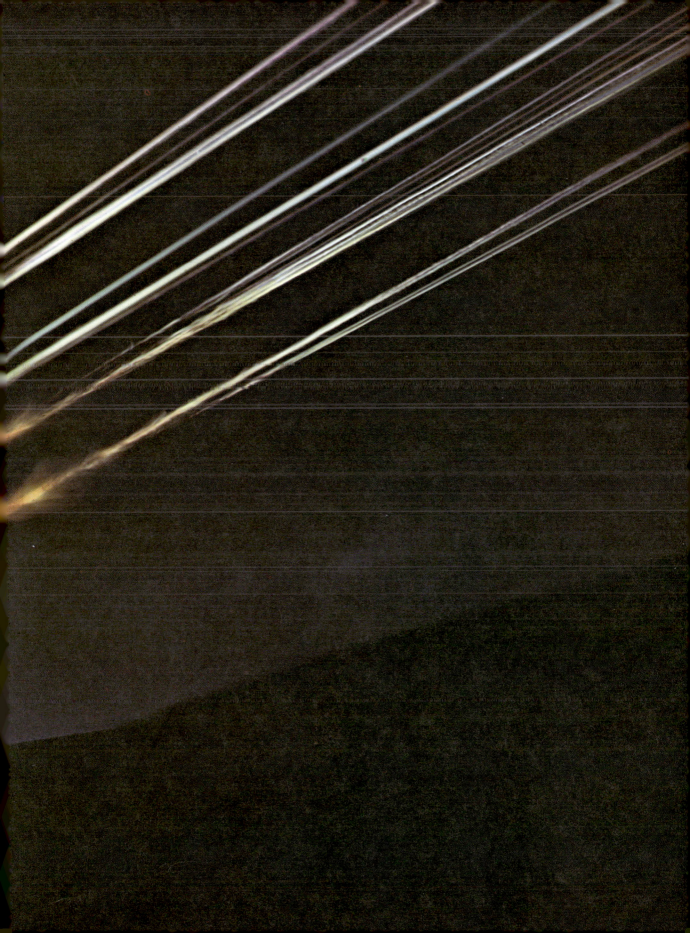

Previous pages: Jerry Vines, the rear gunner in a Halifax crew of R.A.F. Bomber Command, fires his ·303 machine-guns at night for the benefit of the cameraman. *Illustrated* had followed this crew from the start of their training to their first sortie to Berlin. During this period they participated in an operation in the Bay of Biscay, were shot down, and spent $10\frac{1}{2}$ hours in a dinghy before being rescued by a fishing boat. The defensive armament of British heavy bombers was quite inadequate to protect them against night fighters, the rear gunner being in a particularly vulnerable position as many attacks came from that quarter.

Below: Mosquitoes of No. 139 Squadron at Markham on 10 February 1943. Wing Commander W. P. Shand, D.F.C., the commanding officer of the squadron, may be seen in the foreground, in his shirtsleeves, standing in front of Mosquito XD-G: DZ421, which flew with the squadron from January 1943 to April 1944. Mosquito XD-B: DZ373, next in line, was lost over the Scheldt Estuary in March 1943, when it was caught by flak after bombing Liège.

Bombing-up a Mosquito B IV aircraft with 500 lb. bombs. The B IV carried 2,000 lb. of bombs in the fuselage bomb-bay. This picture was taken in February 1943 and shortly afterwards the Mosquito B IX version began to appear, which could carry an extra 1,000 lb. of bombs under the wings. Finally, in March 1944, all Mk IXs and Mk IVs still in service were fitted with bulged bomb-bays to carry the 4,000 lb. 'blockbuster' bomb. The Mosquito was the only light bomber capable of operating with this weapon, which was normally carried by heavy bombers.

Overleaf: De Havilland Mosquito B IV aircraft of No. 139 (Jamaica) Squadron, Royal Air Force Bomber Command, flying in formation on 10 February 1943. During the early years of the war, *The Daily Gleaner*, a Jamaican newspaper, started a fund to buy bombers for Britain. By 1941, Jamaica had contributed enough for twelve Blenheims and, in recognition, Lord Beaverbrook, the Minister of Aircraft Production, decided that Jamaica's name should be linked with a squadron of the R.A.F., thus forging the link with No. 139 Squadron. The squadron had been re-equipped with Mosquitoes by the time this picture was taken.

3 HOME FRONT

In the age of modern total war, the phrase 'the home front' came into use and meant what it implied. With the advent of the bomber and the long-range rocket, everybody came into the firing line and not just those who were unfortunate enough to find themselves in a combat zone. The growth of the 'Nation in Arms' concept during the Napoleonic Wars had led the way to the abandonment of the old, small professional armies and had involved more and more citizens in the defence and security of the state. The Industrial Revolution, with its consequent advances in weapons and their mass production, meant that even those at home were increasingly organized by their governments to keep the armies supplied. However, although their working hours and social habits may have become subject to the government's growing organization of the national war effort, few civilians outside the war zones ran the risk of violent death. Even allowing for the casualties caused by the Zeppelin and Gotha raids in the First World War, the risk of starvation brought about by the U-boat menace resulted in greater hardships, while the German people suffered more from the naval blockade than the limited operations of the Allied bombers in 1918.

The new pattern of warfare between 1939 and 1945 changed all this. With mobility restored to the battlefield, military casualties were less than in the First World War. The British forces suffered some 270,000 fatal casualties, less than half the number of British dead in the 1914-1918 War. The Commonwealth forces lost about 110,000 killed, half the figure of the earlier conflict. Yet 60,000 British civilians died in, or as a result of, air raids as against just over 1,000 in the previous war. The names of Coventry, London, Hamburg, Leningrad, Dresden, Hiroshima and Nagasaki are, in themselves, sufficient to remind us of the new dimension in horror which was added to warfare between 1939 and 1945.

In the face of the common danger, a kind of grass-roots democratic spirit began to emerge in Britain from the Blitz onwards. People no longer relied merely upon the government to organize them; now they began to organize themselves. The air raid warden, factory fire-watcher and Home Guard platoon leader are as symbolic of Britain in the Second World War as the men of Kitchener's New Armies are of the First. It was, as other authors have observed, a 'People's War', at least for a time. However, as the danger receded and victory came nearer, this almost instinctive movement, born out of the need for communal self-preservation, lost its impetus. By 1945 the power and influence of the machinery of state was stronger and more far-reaching than ever before.

The pages of *Illustrated* during the Second World War rarely reflected the full horrors of the conflict. This was inevitable at a time when government censorship and voluntary self-censorship by the press were almost equally prevalent. The photographs in the following pages, which are representative of the kind of pictorial news stories carried by *Illustrated* between 1942 and mid-1944, thus present a stylized and over-glamourized view of Britain at war. Unless one knows their origin, there is little in these pictures to suggest that they were actually taken in wartime. However, this very fact makes them just as typical of the age as the outstanding combat photographs which were taken during the same years. One can learn much about a nation's attitudes during wartime from the type of news which it chooses to publish or chooses not to publish. These pictures show how the British wanted to see themselves or others to see them: happy, confident, and patriotic.

Previous pages (left): King George VI and Queen Elizabeth talking to Air Chief Marshal Lord Dowding outside Buckingham Palace before a Battle of Britain Parade on 26 September 1943. More than 3,000 people, including fighter pilots, anti-aircraft gunners, civil defence and factory workers marched past the King. Earlier in the day, Their Majesties had attended a Thanksgiving Service at St Paul's Cathedral. The King is wearing the uniform of a Marshal of the Royal Air Force. The Queen, according to *The Times,* was wearing 'a coat and halo hat of R.A.F. blue'. Dowding, Commander-in-Chief of Fighter Command from 1936 until late in 1940, was one of the principal architects of victory in the Battle of Britain three years earlier.

Previous pages (right): Proud mothers with their children at a baby show in July 1944. In spite of the rigours of food rationing, the government's special nutritional schemes for mothers and babies were undoubtedly having a beneficial effect by this stage of the war. The infant mortality rate in England and Wales dropped from fifty-one in every thousand in 1939 to forty-six per thousand by 1945. The Ministry of Food's Vitamin Welfare Scheme, introduced in December 1941, provided free cod-liver oil and blackcurrant juice for under-twos, although Lend-lease orange juice, for which a small charge was made, later replaced the blackcurrant. However, through ignorance or indifference, British mothers failed to take full advantage of the scheme, only a quarter of the scheduled issue of cod-liver oil being taken up in 1944.

The photographs on these and the next two pages were taken by the *Illustrated* cameraman at a 'United Nations' Christmas party in 1942. The party was given by Petty Officer Roy Silas of the Royal Naval Patrol Service at his home at East Sheen in the London suburbs. Here, Allied men and women get together for a sing-song. Apart from members of the British Services, the guests also included men and women from America, Russia, Poland, Norway, and Holland. The beaming host is in the centre wearing a topee. A Dutch sailor sports a yellow paper hat. The Polish sailor (in a green paper hat) has his arm around a Norwegian Wren. A U.S. Marine in the right corner hides behind an A.T.S. corporal.

Olejnik Kazimierz, a Polish sailor (left) and Private First Class M. Miller of the United States Marines chat with leading Aircraftwoman Olive Glover, a W.A.A.F., and Corporal Reed of the A.T.S. On the wall behind them is a portrait of Captain E. S. F. Fegen, R.N., who was awarded a posthumous V.C. for his action in November 1940 when commanding the armed merchant cruiser *Jervis Bay*. Fegen went down with his ship while defending a convoy against the German pocket battleship *Admiral Scheer*. The portrait was done by Iris Silas, in whose home the party was being held.

This group is less inhibited in its expression of friendship than the one above. The international embraces involve two G.I.s, Tamara Eidus from Russia (left), and a girl whose nationality is less apparent than her good nature.

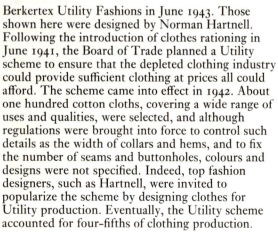

Berkertex Utility Fashions in June 1943. Those shown here were designed by Norman Hartnell. Following the introduction of clothes rationing in June 1941, the Board of Trade planned a Utility scheme to ensure that the depleted clothing industry could provide sufficient clothing at prices all could afford. The scheme came into effect in 1942. About one hundred cotton cloths, covering a wide range of uses and qualities, were selected, and although regulations were brought into force to control such details as the width of collars and hems, and to fix the number of seams and buttonholes, colours and designs were not specified. Indeed, top fashion designers, such as Hartnell, were invited to popularize the scheme by designing clothes for Utility production. Eventually, the Utility scheme accounted for four-fifths of clothing production.

A female war-worker poses for a pin-up picture while on holiday in Cornwall in September 1943. *Illustrated* reported that Britain's boarding houses and hotels at seaside resorts were packed to capacity as late as October and November of that year.

Right: Star of the war years: a pin-up photograph of actress Anne Crawford, taken by Jarché at the Shepherds Bush studios of Gainsborough Pictures Ltd on 27 April 1944. Anne Crawford, whose real name was Imelda Crawford, was born in 1920 and, after training at the Royal Academy of Dramatic Art and in repertory, made her film debut for Herbert Wilcox and Warner Brothers in the 1942 film *They Flew Alone*. She made some seventeen films between 1942 and 1954, including such box-office successes as *Millions Like Us* (for Gainsborough Pictures in 1943) and *Master of Bankdam* (1947).

Eighty-three year old Tom Beasley, then the oldest swordsmith in England, forges the blade of the Stalingrad Sword, 1 July 1943. Early in 1943, King George VI had agreed to a suggestion that he should confer an award on the people of Stalingrad in recognition of their prolonged and gallant resistance to the Germans. It was eventually decided that a Sword of Honour should be prepared at the King's command and suitably embellished and inscribed as a gift from His Majesty to Stalingrad as a token of the admiration of the British people. The King finally selected a design by R. M. Y. Gleadowe for a two-handed, two-edged sword, of hardest steel, inscribed: 'To the steel-hearted citizens of Stalingrad, the gift of King George VI, in token of the homage of the British people'. Tom Beasley, seen here wearing a traditional swordsmith's bonnet, left hospital after an operation to forge the blade for the Wilkinson Sword Co. of Chiswick.

Corporal Leslie Durbin of the Royal Air Force, a peacetime silversmith, fixes the Royal Coat of Arms and Cypher to the gold- and silver-decorated scabbard of the Stalingrad Sword, having been given special leave from the R.A.F. for the purpose. When finished, the Sword of Honour was exhibited in various British cities and some half-a-million people, many having queued for hours, saw it during its tour. Corporal Durbin accompanied the sword on the tour. It was presented to Stalin by Churchill at the Teheran Conference on 29 November 1943, and was later placed, on Stalin's order, in the War Museum of the rebuilt city of Stalingrad.

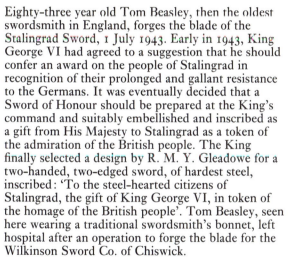

Babies at a wartime day nursery at Hatfield in June 1943. As the number of working mothers increased during the war, the provision of state-sponsored nurseries was greatly expanded. There were some 1,450 such nurseries, under local authorities, by the end of 1943, with places for 65,000 children under five. However, it proved difficult to find sufficient suitable staff for the nurseries, and many mothers preferred to leave their children with neighbours or relatives while they were at work.

4 PERSONNEL

If nothing else, war makes it easier to study the human race. Both the worst and best aspects of human nature emerge under the stress of war. During conflicts between nations many individuals have discovered themselves and their fellows for the first time. Experiences are heightened, the senses sharpened and hidden strengths and weaknesses come to the fore. It is no accident that those who took part in the First and Second World Wars often remember them as the most exhilarating experience in their lives, the time when, in the face of death, they discovered the true meaning of comradeship and became aware of what was really important to them. Apathy and indifference tend to disappear with war.

In these photographs we are given a brief glimpse of individuals at war, ranging from the men who commanded one of the greatest operations in the history of warfare down to ordinary soldiers, sailors, and airmen. Although these pictures all depict Allied servicemen, their moods, desires and fears were common to men of every belligerent nation.

At the highest level of command, Eisenhower and Mountbatten, both of whom appear in these pages, were responsible for the direction of forces of unprecedented size and scope in campaigns which were as diverse as their own personalities and backgrounds. Both had multi-national forces under their command and both had to integrate the operations of land, sea and air forces into the overall strategic plan. In as much as the European theatre was the agreed priority in Allied strategy, Eisenhower was better provided with the tools for victory but because he was both a Supreme Allied Commander and an American, he was often faced with the difficult problem of reconciling profound differences of opinion as to how the campaign in north-west Europe should be conducted. This came to a head in the disagreement with Montgomery over the question of whether the Allies should concentrate on a single thrust into Germany or advance on a broad front following the defeat of the German forces in France in the summer of 1944. Historians still disagree as to who was right, but what is certain is that few commanders could have retained firm control over a team which included such incompatible personalities as Montgomery and Patton and still lead it to victory, after weathering the crisis of the German offensive in the Ardennes. Eisenhower may not have been the most dynamic leader or the most perceptive strategist of the war, but few could match his ability as a co-ordinator or his tactful handling of subordinates. Mountbatten's style of leadership was essentially more dynamic and personal even if many of his problems were the same. His success as Supreme Allied Commander, South-East Asia, lay at least partly in the extent to which he was able to revitalize a theatre in which the soldiers believed themselves 'forgotten'. But he too faced his difficulties as a team leader. If Eisenhower had his Montgomery, and his Patton, Mountbatten had his Stilwell and his Chiang-Kai-Shek.

At the other end of the scale, the common soldier, sailor or airman of the Second World War, while called upon to perform feats or endure hardships equal to anything his father or grandfather may have experienced, was rarely sent, completely uncomprehending, into battle. Not only did the new techniques of warfare ensure that the wholesale slaughter of Verdun and the Somme was not repeated; they also called for a higher degree of sophistication and skill from those who were required to operate or implement them. As the massive frontal assaults against trenches and machine-guns gave way to 'blitzkrieg' tactics, so commanders were obliged to take their men more and more into their confidence. Better-educated and more socially-conscious than previous generations of fighting men, the men of the Second World War at least had a clearer idea than their predecessors, of what they were doing and why they were doing it. This trend is illustrated by the two pictures of aircrew being briefed before sorties over enemy-occupied territory. Of all types of operation in the Second World War, offensive air operations called for more detailed briefing of individual participants than almost any other form of warfare. In some ways, these two photographs sum up the difference between the two World Wars better than many others in this book, especially in relation to the role which the individual was allowed, or thought he was being allowed, to play.

Previous pages (left): Pilots of No. 453 Squadron, an Australian Spitfire Squadron of the Second Tactical Air Force, are briefed at their airfield at Ford in May 1944, shortly before D-Day. Flying Spitfire IXBs, they formed part of 125 Wing (83 Group) at Ford, near Chichester. Following the Normandy landings, 83 Group squadrons were to provide fighter cover for the forward troops as they advanced inland. No. 453 Squadron was one of the units assigned to low-level beachhead cover. On D-Day they were to remain on patrol for 50 minutes at a time at a height of 3,000-5,000 feet. In the week before D-Day they carried out fighter-bomber attacks on German radar stations at Cap D'Antifer, Cap Gris Nez and Arromanches. They also dive-bombed railway targets at Douai. They moved to an advanced airstrip in Normandy on 25 June 1944.

Previous pages (right): Major-General E. A. E. Tremlett (with the red tabs on his collar) and members of his staff at Anti-Aircraft Control Headquarters in London on 7 February 1943. The controlling 'master-mind' behind London's anti-aircraft barrage, Tremlett is sitting on a raised platform in the gun control room, deep below ground in central London. On his desk is a microphone through which he can give orders direct to the anti-aircraft batteries defending the capital. He is watching girls of the A.T.S. (Auxiliary Territorial Service) plotting aircraft movements. The officer nearest the camera is controlling the height of fire and the type of shells to be used. During the period when this picture was taken, the Luftwaffe were carrying out their first major attacks on British targets since 1941, largely, however, without success.

Overleaf: Photographed on 14 February 1944, the men who planned and directed Operation Overlord, the Allied invasion of north-west Europe, through Normandy, in June 1944. They are (from left to right): Lieutenant-General Omar N. Bradley (commanding First United States Army); Admiral Sir Bertram Ramsay (commanding Allied Naval Expeditionary Force); Air Chief Marshal Sir Arthur Tedder (Deputy Supreme Commander, Allied Expeditionary Force); General Dwight D. Eisenhower (Supreme Commander); General Sir Bernard Montgomery (commanding 21st Army Group); Air Chief Marshal Sir Trafford Leigh-Mallory (commanding Allied Expeditionary Air Force); and Lieutenant-General Walter Bedell Smith (Chief of Staff). There was no single command for all the Allied air forces. The strategic bombing forces of R.A.F. Bomber Command, the United States Army Air Forces in Britain and the Mediterranean were ultimately responsible to the Combined Chiefs of Staff, but for Overlord they were placed under Eisenhower's operational control. The co-ordination of all air forces, strategic and tactical, was entrusted by Eisenhower to Tedder.

General Sir Bernard Montgomery (now Field-Marshal the Viscount Montgomery of Alamein), who commanded the British 21st Army Group in the campaign in north-west Europe, 1944-45, is seen here addressing officers and N.C.O.s of the 50th (Northumbrian) Division in a Normandy field in July 1944. During June and July, this division, which had landed on Gold Beach, on the right flank of the British Second Army on D-Day, was involved in bitter fighting against the German Panzer Lehr Division in the struggle for Tilly-sur-Seulles and Villers-Bocage. Their divisional flashes are clearly visible on their battledress sleeves, the double 'T' motif standing for the Rivers Tyne and Tees. Montgomery is wearing his famous black beret, first given to him by a tank regiment in the Western Desert, before El Alamein, when he commanded the Eighth Army. As he explained in his memoirs, what was at first a private joke later became the means by which he was instantly recognized.

Air Chief Marshal Sir Arthur Harris, Commander-in-Chief, R.A.F. Bomber Command since 1942, is seen here with members of his staff at Bomber Command Headquarters, High Wycombe, on 27 February 1944. He is examining target photographs, taken by Allied photographic reconnaissance aircraft and now subject to the closest scrutiny in the H.Q.'s Bombing Interpretation Room. During this period of the strategic bombing offensive against Germany, Bomber Command was engaged in what became known as the Battle of Berlin, a massive campaign at the heart of which were sixteen major attacks against Berlin between 18 November 1943 and 24 March 1944. However, because of the growing ascendancy of the German night fighter defences during these months, the night area offensive directed by Harris was coming close to defeat in the face of prohibitive casualty rates. Only a few nights before, on 19/20 February, Bomber Command had lost 120 aircraft in attacks on Berlin

and Leipzig out of a total of 1,691 sorties. Subsequent attacks on targets in southern Germany, including Stuttgart (20/21), Schweinfurt (24/25) and Augsburg (26/27) had resulted in lighter losses (63 aircraft from 1,307 sorties) mainly because of less intense defences on the southern route. Yet, only a few months later, as the Allied long-range escort fighters began to defeat the Luftwaffe in the daylight air offensive, Bomber Command was able to mount devastating area and precision attacks by both night and day, against a wide variety of targets, with relatively light losses.

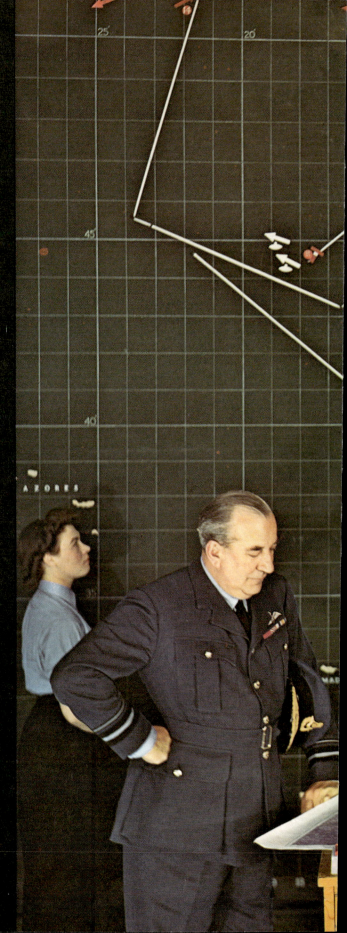

Air Marshal Sir John Slessor, Commander-in-Chief, R.A.F. Coastal Command from February 1943 to January 1944 (seen in the foreground, centre) at Coastal Command Headquarters at Northwood in Middlesex, September 1943. With him in the Operations Room are Air Vice-Marshal A. Durston (left), his Senior Air Staff Officer, and Captain D. V. Peyton-Ward (right), his Senior Naval Staff Officer. During Slessor's tenure of office, Coastal Command's main priority was the defeat of the U-boat in the Battle of the Atlantic. Slessor held command throughout the peak year during which the German submarine menace was largely overcome and a record number of U-boats destroyed (Coastal Command destroying 84 out of 219). Slessor considered the Bay of Biscay to be the most likely place to find U-boats moving to and from their French bases on their Atlantic missions, and concentrated his attack in this area, the 'trunk of the Atlantic U-boat menace' as he called it. Between April and August, aircraft of Coastal Command sank twenty-five submarines in this area. In the background a W.A.A.F. (Women's Auxiliary Air Force) is plotting movements in the Bay of Biscay on the large wall map. She is wearing a special safety harness which will lower her gently to the floor should she slip.

Previous pages: Royal Marines from ships of the East Indies Fleet prepare to cross a river during jungle warfare training in Ceylon, January 1945. It had been decided to use them to capture Cheduba, an island off the Burma coast, 100 miles south of Akyab, and this picture was taken during their one month's training for the task. The Cheduba operation was to help gain full control of the waters around Ramree, where the Allies intended to establish an air base for the supply of the 14th Army in its advance down central Burma. The landings on Cheduba, by 500 Royal Marines, took place on 26 January. Although stiff opposition was expected, in the event there were only a few Japanese left on the island. Re-embarked on 28 January, they manned the guns of the cruisers during the bombardment of Ramree the same afternoon, causing their commanding officer to remark that it was doubtful if so rapid a switch from land to sea to land and back again to sea could be found throughout the regiment's history.

Left above: A Gurkha with his kukri or fighting knife. Although they have been familiar and popular figures in the British and Indian Armies for well over a century, Gurkhas, the soldiers of Nepal, have never been subjects of the Crown. In spite of the bonds of affection and loyalty binding them to Britain, they have, in fact, been enlisted as mercenaries. They trace their origin to a small region and a single town in Nepal, Gorakha or Gorkha, 50 miles from Katmandu. The anglicized spelling Gurkha has long been adopted for all soldiers from Nepal, although many of them come from different areas of the country. Defeated by the British in the war against Nepal from 1814 to 1816, both sides quickly gained respect for each other and the first Nepalese hillmen were being recruited into British forces before the end of 1816. Over the next hundred years some twenty Gurkha rifle battalions were established and became a kind of 'corps d'élite' in the British Indian Army. Some 10,000 Gurkhas died during the Second World War, but ten V.C.s were won by them during that conflict. The kukri, the national weapon of Nepal, became a deadly fighting knife in the hands of the Gurkha. Many myths have grown up around it – for instance, that it is never unsheathed without drawing blood. However, although it is a formidable weapon, it is also used widely for mundane tasks such as chopping wood, slaughtering poultry and opening cans. With its two miniature knives sheathed to the rear of the main blade and used for sharpening and skinning, it is carried by nearly all Nepalese hillmen.

Left below: Sepoy Bhandari Ram of the 16th/10th Baluch Regiment, with his father, shortly after receiving his Victoria Cross from Lord Wavell at an investiture in India in February 1945. On 8 November 1944, Mountbatten had ordered an offensive to be launched to clear north Arakan in Burma, to be known as Operation Romulus. This was to be completed by the end of January 1945. While the plan was being prepared, the 25th Indian Infantry Division infiltrated forward to secure jumping-off points for the general advance. They cleared the coastal plain in the Godusara area, and, on the eastern side of the Mayu Range, established an outpost line astride the Maungdaw–Buthidaung Road. The 16th/10th Baluch Regiment had to take over and hold a number of points in the Mayu sector. Running into heavy opposition in trying to capture a feature known as Office, a company led by Major M. Usman made a brilliant dash to capture it. Bhandari Ram, though wounded, crawled up to a Japanese machine-gun and, disregarding further wounds, killed the gunner and two others, inspiring the rest of his platoon to rush the position. His was one of thirty V.C.s won by the Indian Army during the Second World War.

Admiral Lord Louis Mountbatten (now Admiral of the Fleet the Earl Mountbatten of Burma) takes the wheel of a Jeep during a tour of military installations in Ceylon in November 1944. Mountbatten was then Supreme Allied Commander, South-East Asia.

Wing Commander W. P. Shand briefing aircrew of No. 139 (Jamaica) Squadron, R.A.F. Bomber Command, on 10 February 1943, at Markham. Shand is at the far end of the room in his shirtsleeves. The squadron, recently equipped with Mosquito IV bombers, was then forging, with other squadrons of No. 2 Group, the methods of attack known as 'shallow-dive formation' and 'low-level formation'. The two formations co-ordinated their attacks to cause the maximum confusion to the enemy defences the 'shallow-divers' diving from 2,000 ft and releasing their bombs at 1,500 ft, whilst the low-level aircraft went across the target at the lowest possible height. Flights to and from the target were made at ground level, calling for expert navigation. In the hands of the 2 Group squadrons, the Mosquito's ability to destroy pinpoint targets became almost legendary. A few days earlier, on 31 January, No. 139 Squadron carried out one of the first Mosquito attacks on Berlin, and in the fortnight following this photograph attacked an armaments works at Liège, engine sheds at Tours, and U-boat stores at Rennes. In the summer of 1943, the squadron went over to night operations with the Pathfinder Force. In 1944 it became an H2S-equipped Mosquito marker squadron and took part in many attacks carrying 4,000 lb. bombs as well as target indicators. In February and March 1945 it made thirty-six consecutive attacks on Berlin. During the war it flew some 4,000 sorties and dropped some 1,500 tons of bombs. Shand himself was shot down over the Dutch coast by a fighter during a nuisance raid on Berlin in April 1943.

'Dad's Army'. Men of the Home Guard demonstrate the art of camouflage for the *Illustrated* photographer in August 1943. From the insignia visible in the picture the men appear to belong to the 25th Battalion London Home Guard, which had started as a unit of Local Defence Volunteers in July 1940, at Blackheath. It therefore seems likely that the picture was taken at Blackheath. The larger weapon in the centre of the photograph is a 29 mm. Spigot Mortar known as the Blacker Bombard, one of the strange variety of weapons with which the Home Guard was equipped. It is armed with an anti-tank round.

Royal Marines and sailors help to bath a marine on the deck of a sea fort in the Thames Estuary, November 1944. Early in 1941, work started on the construction of forts which could be sunk in the approaches to the Thames and would be provided with heavy anti-aircraft weapons. The first of them was in position by February 1942 and by August there were two in the Thames and two off Harwich, all manned by naval crews. In addition, there were three similar forts manned by the army. With the shore guns of Anti-Aircraft Command, the fighters of Nos. 11 and 12 Groups and the coastal radar stations, they played a part in helping to frustrate German attempts to interfere with traffic in and out of the Port of London. They were known as Maunsell Forts after their designer, Guy Maunsell. Equipped with light and heavy anti-aircraft guns, searchlights and radar, they were placed at strategic points to combat enemy mining operations in the Thames, to watch for E-boats, to contribute to Air Sea Rescue services, and to help maintain off-shore convoy communications. They came into their own with the resumption of enemy mine-laying in 1943 and with the advent of the flying-bombs in 1944.

Right: A Leading Stoker drawing his fire aboard a trawler of the Royal Naval Patrol Service, in March 1943. Apart from helping to provide the power for the craft, the stoker also had to be careful not to make too much smoke, as, even with the advent of radar, an early sighting by an enemy vessel or aircraft could prove fatal.

5 THE AMERICANS

By the late spring of 1944, just before the launching of Operation Overlord, the vast majority of the 1,421,000 Allied, Dominion and colonial servicemen and women, who had somehow been crowded into the United Kingdom, were, in fact, American. This, in itself, reflected the dominance of the United States in the Anglo-American partnership by that date. The very presence of so many Americans on British soil could not but help having some effect on the British way of life. But it is misleading to exaggerate the effects of the American presence on British society during the Second World War. In many respects, the G.I.s formed a self-contained community and enjoyed comforts and facilities denied to the inhabitants of wartime Britain, who were forced to endure rationing and utility goods. Candy, cigarettes and nylon stockings were available in ample quantities from the P.X., and American servicemen had their own films, newspapers, and radio services. Though these factors did not prevent the cementing of Anglo-American friendship, and a certain measure of mutual integration, the sheer quantity of material and the quality of the equipment and comforts with which they were provided, inevitably made the Americans the object of some hostility and envy. A 1943 Mass Observation survey revealed that the Americans in the United Kingdom were less popular than, for example, the Czechs. An oft-quoted phrase of the time described the 'Yanks' as 'over-paid, over-sexed and over here'.

Among the longest-serving American residents of the United Kingdom were the men of the United States Eighth Army Air Force. Operating mainly from bases in East Anglia, they represented the major part of the American contribution to the Allied strategic air offensive against Germany. American bombing doctrine was based on the concept of daylight precision bombing by unescorted and heavily-armed four-engined bombers flying in tight and mutually-supporting defensive combat formations. Though the experience of R.A.F. Bomber Command before 1942 had exposed the fallacy of the unescorted daylight attack, the Americans persisted in this belief between their first tentative missions in the late summer of 1942 until the autumn of 1943. The prohibitive losses which were by then being suffered, particularly in two disastrous missions to the ball-bearings factories at Schweinfurt (August and October 1943), led them to speed up the large-scale production of long-range escort fighters which could fly with the bombers deep into the heart of the Reich and force the Luftwaffe on to the defensive. The most successful of these fighters was the P 51 Mustang, a successful marriage of an American airframe with the Rolls-Royce Merlin engine, built under licence by Packard. The Mustang, which had the performance of an interceptor and the range of a bomber, was a major factor in the winning of air superiority over Germany in 1944. Equipped with long-range fuel tanks, it was originally used to protect the bombers but soon became a potent offensive weapon. Fighter and bomber operations became complementary, the bombers acting as bait to draw up the Luftwaffe, whose fighters could then be shot out of the sky by the Mustangs, Thunderbolts and Lightnings of the Eighth Air Force. By the spring of 1944, the Allies had largely won command of the air and this had immeasurable influence on the success of Overlord and its preliminary tactical air operations. Thereafter, both the Royal Air Force and the United States Army Air Forces were able to bring their full weight to bear on the Reich and its industries.

It is perhaps fitting that the following photographs should include pictures of the men and machines of the 4th Fighter Group. Not only was this Group the highest-scoring fighter unit in the Eighth Air Force but also many of its original members had flown with the Royal Air Force Eagle Squadrons, formed from American volunteers before the United States had entered the war. When they had transferred to the VIII Fighter Command in 1942, the men of the 4th Fighter Group had been reluctant to exchange their Spitfires for the heavier P 47 Thunderbolt which other groups, particularly the 56th, were to fly with great success. It was not until the 4th received the Mustang in February 1944 that they began to establish their claim as the leading fighter group in the European theatre of operations.

Also reflected in these pages is the American occupation of Iceland. The occupation of Iceland, first by British and Canadian, and then by American forces, must be among the few examples in the history of warfare of one country actually asking others to occupy it. Iceland held a vital strategic position as a link in communications between Britain and North America, and aircraft based there could cover a portion of the North Atlantic shipping routes. The Germans were known to have cast their eyes towards Iceland as a potential naval and air base in their plan for pre-eminence in the Atlantic. To deter a possible German invasion and to preserve the country's freedom, British and Canadian contingents were brought in to defend Iceland by the end of July 1940. Even before America entered the war, Roosevelt had negotiated an agreement with the Icelandic government whereby the protection of Iceland would be entrusted to American troops, relieving the British detachments for service elsewhere. The American occupation began in July 1941, and by mid-1942, their forces totalled over 20,000, although the protection of the barren country, with its 2,500 miles of exposed coastline, involved the wide dispersal of troops.

The role of the United States Navy in the Second World War is illustrated, in a way, by the photographs of the U.S.S. *Arkansas*. As the U.S. Navy's main concern was with the Pacific theatre, it is understandable that the *Illustrated* photographers did not often have the opportunity to reflect its world-wide role. The extent to which the U.S. Navy, in the person of Admiral King, its Commander-in-Chief and Chief of Naval Staff, managed to modify the original strategic principle that the European theatre should take priority over the Pacific, is one of the most interesting aspects of Allied strategy during the war. That it succeeded may be gauged from the fact that, by the end of 1943, there were as many American servicemen in the Pacific as in the European theatre. The *Arkansas* herself reflected this strategic debate for, after undertaking convoy duties in the Atlantic and forming part of the naval forces which supported the Normandy beachhead, she went out to the Pacific and participated in the operations related to the landings on Iwo Jima in February and March 1945. The *Arkansas* also symbolized a vanishing era. Built before the First World War, she, like all other battleships, was rendered obsolete by the growing influence of air power on naval operations and the emergence of the aircraft carrier as the new type of capital ship.

Previous pages (left): Lieutenant-Colonel James A. Clark, Deputy Commander of the American 4th Fighter Group, briefs pilots at Debden before a 'Jackpot' (airfield strafing) mission to southern France on 10 April 1944. On this mission, the Group scored twenty-eight 'kills', bringing their total victory score to over 400 enemy aircraft destroyed. Clark is in the centre of the picture with a map on his knees. Among the other 'aces' in the photograph are Captain Don S. Gentile (on Clark's left, holding cap) and Major James A. Goodson (seated on Clark's immediate right).

Previous pages (right): Captain Don S. Gentile on the wing of his P-51 B Mustang 'Shangri-La' at Debden on 10 April 1944. Gentile, a member of the famous 4th Fighter Group, became one of the leading 'aces' of the Eighth Air Force, gaining 21.8 victories in aerial combat and destroying 6 aircraft on the ground by the end of April 1944, when he returned to the United States. Having already learned to fly, he volunteered for service with the Royal Air Force in 1940, and flew with No. 133 Eagle Squadron, composed of American volunteers, in 1942 before transferring to the Eighth Air Force in September of that year. Over half his victories were scored in April 1944. After a spell as a test pilot, he re-entered the U.S.A.F. after the war and was killed in a flying accident in 1951. All 4th Fighter Group Mustangs carried the distinctive red nose and spinner markings seen here. This particular aircraft was wrecked on 13 April 1944, when Gentile flew too low as he 'buzzed' Debden.

Two parka-clad G.I.s pose with a local beauty by the side of an open-air hot-spring swimming pool at Reykjavik, Iceland, in October 1943.

Top: An American soldier on lonely sentry duty by a trench in the bleak landscape of Iceland, in October 1943.

Standing on the port wing of the P-47 Thunderbolt
fighter 'Spokane Chief', Peggy Diggins, American
War Correspondent and photographer, takes a
picture of Major Eugene P. Roberts, who is seated in
the cockpit of his aircraft. Roberts, who commanded
the 84th Fighter Squadron of the 78th Fighter
Group at Duxford, where this picture was taken in
September 1943, had recently become the second
Eighth Air Force fighter pilot to destroy five enemy
aircraft and gain the coveted status of an 'ace'. In
doing so, he had also become the first American pilot
to shoot down three aircraft on a single mission (two
Fw 190s and an Me 109 on 30 July).

Staff Sergeant Frank T. Lusic, an air gunner of the B-17 Flying Fortress 'Meat Hound' of the United States Eighth Army Air Force, prepares for a mission on 4 May 1943. Earlier, he had put on an electrically-heated woollen suit, a wool-lined leather flying suit, two pairs of gloves and his Mae West and parachute. Such clothing was necessary to protect him against the sub-zero temperatures at the altitudes at which the B-17 groups usually operated. On this particular day, 79 B-17s bombed the Ford and General Motors works at Antwerp, suffering no losses. The B-17 with which the Eighth Air Force bomber groups were largely equipped at this time carried nine to eleven ·50 machine guns, in nose, dorsal, waist ball turret (beneath the fuselage) and tail positions. It is likely that this picture was taken at the Thurleigh base of the 306th Bomb Group, one of the first four B-17 groups to operate from England.

A ground crew at the East Anglian base of a heavy bomber group of the United States Eighth Army Air Force collect empty ·50 calibre shell cases from a B-17 Flying Fortress which had just returned from a mission over Germany on 6 September 1943. Several thousand rounds had been fired by the gunners of this aircraft in the air battle over Europe that day. The Eighth Air Force bombardment groups, still without long-range fighter escort in their missions over Germany during these months, were in the middle of the most critical period of the daylight bombing offensive and were suffering prohibitive losses at the hands of the Luftwaffe in massive air battles, to which this picture testifies. The B-17 in this photograph had just returned from the disastrous mission to the instrument bearing factory at Stuttgart. The Luftwaffe controllers had concentrated and marshalled their fighters with great skill and some bomber groups were decimated by head-on attacks. Heavy clouds also dispersed the bomber force and of 338 aircraft which set out, over half were forced to seek other targets, forty-five bombers were lost on the mission. Note the ball turret under the fuselage.

Following pages 1: Dawn breaks over a convoy in the Atlantic Ocean, as seen from the American battleship, U.S.S. *Arkansas*, in February 1944. The *Arkansas* had left New York on 19 January, escorting a convoy to Bangor in Northern Ireland, returning to the United States by 14 February. Note the 20 mm. anti-aircraft guns in the foreground. The *Arkansas* carried over thirty of these weapons by the end of the war.

Following pages 2: View of the main deck of the battleship U.S.S. *Arkansas*, in the Atlantic, in February 1944. The camera is situated amidships, looking forward. Note the Vought OS2U-3 Kingfisher floatplane on its catapult on the roof of one of the ship's 12-inch turrets. This two-seat observation-scout monoplane became the work horse of the American fleets. Among its tasks were those of spotting for naval gunfire, reconnaissance, anti-submarine patrols, shipping attacks and liaison work. It had a range of some 900 miles.

Following pages 3: Anti-aircraft gun positions on board the U.S.S. *Arkansas* in February 1944. In the foreground can be seen two twin-40 mm. mountings. Below these are two of the ship's 3-inch anti-aircraft guns, and, just visible above the waves, are two 5-inch guns, part of the secondary armament of the *Arkansas*. The main armament of this battleship comprised twelve 12-inch guns mounted in six turrets. By 1945, all the secondary main deck guns had been removed and the anti-aircraft armament increased to ten 3-inch, twenty-four 40 mm. and over thirty 20 mm. guns.

6 WOMEN AT WAR

Between 1914 and 1918 the number of women and girls working in British industry rose by some 800,000 from 2,179,000 to 2,971,000. If the professions, nursing, the auxiliary police force, railways, agriculture, and the new women's Services are taken into account, nearly 2,000,000 women entered paid employment for the first time, bringing the total of working women to some 7,500,000. The general contribution of women to the national war effort did more to win them political and social emancipation than all the activities of the militant suffragettes before the war. On the other hand, real economic emancipation remained as remote as equal pay and a large proportion of them left the factories as quickly as they entered them, once the national crisis was over. However, a slow rise in the number of women in industry was resumed between the wars, while some branches of industry, such as the textile mills, had long relied on women to supply a substantial part of their labour force. Twenty-one years later, British industry was as ill-prepared for a long war as it had been in 1914, and by July 1941 the manpower shortage was assuming critical proportions. It was calculated that, by the following June, the forces and munitions industries would be at least 300,000 men and women short of requirements, while Churchill's insistence on an increase in the bomber building programme would involve an estimated 850,000 extra workers. This situation led the War Cabinet, on 2 December 1941, to announce the conscription of women, a measure which was not systematically adopted in any other country, not even in Soviet Russia or Nazi Germany. Single women between twenty (later nineteen) and thirty were to be called up and would have a choice between serving in the auxiliary services or in industry. That this momentous step should have met so little opposition was due to Bevin's skill and tact in administering the scheme and the general willingness of the people to co-operate in the national interest. The Wartime Social Survey showed that 97 per cent of British women were agreed that women should undertake war work.

By mid-1944, some 10,000,000 women were still tied to the household, many of them looking after young children or old people. 1,000,000 were participating in various voluntary organizations, such as the W.V.S., or in Civil Defence. However, the proportion of women in the forces and industry was double that of 1918 and twice as many married women were now working as had been before 1939. Of the 18–40 age group, 90 per cent of single girls and 80 per cent of married women were in the Services or factories. Some of the remainder became 'out-workers', producing small components in their own sitting rooms. Girls who, before the war would have worked in offices or shops, now went into the Services, ordnance factories, or the Women's Land Army. Older women, less mobile because of greater domestic ties, took their places in the factories, shops and offices in their own neighbourhood. Although a very large proportion of these working women went into lighter engineering, heavier jobs were by no means beyond them. They proved particularly adept at tasks such as welding, while about 100,000 found employment on the railways, some even acting as porters. Over 1,500,000 served in the engineering and metal industries. Of the younger women, more than 450,000 were in the forces by mid 1944. Their duties mainly lay in the spheres of clerical or communications work, but many were exposed to considerable dangers as, for example, nurses in combat zones, as plotters in the operations rooms of fighter stations, or as members of the mixed searchlight and anti-aircraft batteries of Anti-Aircraft Command.

To most working women, faced with long hours, shift work and dull repetitive jobs, money was the chief attraction, especially if their husbands were in the forces. On the railways or buses, the average wage was over £4 a week by 1945; women in engineering received about £1 less in their pay-packets. Nevertheless, most men in industry earned at least twice as much as women. Most employers found loopholes in the industrial agreements of 1940-42 which aimed at moving towards the concept of equal pay. Although the major trade unions reported large increases in female membership, the number of women in unions doubling to over 1,800,000 by 1944, the problem of inequality of pay remained.

Whereas women had received the vote following their effort in the First World War, they received no similar reward, in terms of full economic emancipation, after the Second World War. What the 1939-45 conflict did do, however, was to heighten the social self-confidence and independence towards which women had been progressing ever since the First World War had blown away the rigid social patterns of Victorian and Edwardian society. The 'pill' and the mini-skirt, with their implied release of women from their previously subordinate position in society, stem directly from the trend towards female emancipation which was given major impetus during the World Wars. Whether the Women's Liberation movement in the 1970s would agree that the battle has really been won is another matter.

Previous pages (right): The Countess of Limerick (seated left) and Lady Louis Mountbatten in December 1942. The Countess of Limerick was then Deputy Chairman of the Executive Committee of the Joint War Organization of the British Red Cross Society and the Order of St John, while Lady Louis Mountbatten had been Superintendent-in-Chief of the Nursing Corps and Divisions of the St John Ambulance Brigade since the previous July, and was also a member of the Executive Committee of the Joint War Organization. The Joint War Organization did much magnificent work for the relief of suffering, both military and civilian, during the war, concerning itself with the welfare of the wounded, prisoners of war, air-raid casualties, and relatives of the missing as well as the civilian victims of the famine and disease which followed in the wake of war, both in Europe and elsewhere. Both women played a major part in this work. The Countess of Limerick's duties in supervising the far-flung activities of the British Red Cross took her to countries as far apart as Egypt and the United States. Lady Mountbatten was able to make perhaps her greatest contribution after her husband had been appointed Supreme Allied Commander, South-East Asia in 1943. In 1945 she inaugurated desperately needed welfare services for Allied prisoners of war and internees in a gigantic rescue operation covering the whole of south-east Asia following the Japanese surrender. After the war, when Lord Mountbatten was the last Viceroy and the first Governor-General of independent India, she made prodigious efforts to stem the tide of suffering caused by the massacres and migrations of whole populations in the Punjab, serving as Chairman of the United Council for Relief and Welfare. In 1950 she became Superintendent-in-Chief of the St John Ambulance Brigade Overseas, involving long and exhausting tours of inspection. She died in February 1960, in North Borneo, during one of her overseas tours.

Previous pages (left): Private Mary Caterer of Falmouth, tenor drummer in the A.T.S. band in November 1942.

Air Commandant Lady Welsh, Director, Women's Auxiliary Air Force (seated left) with the Deputy Director, Group Officer I. M. Campbell, in December 1943. Born Ruth Mary Eldred Dalzell in 1896, Lady Welsh had driven an ambulance in France during the First World War. She married Squadron Leader W. L. Welsh (later Air Marshal Sir William Welsh) in 1922. Volunteering for service in the A.T.S. (Auxiliary Training Service) in 1938, she transferred to the W.A.A.F. in September 1939. As a staff officer at the Air Ministry, at Command and at Group headquarters, and finally as Inspector, she gained a wide experience of the work and conditions of the W.A.A.F. before succeeding Air Chief Commandant K. J. T. Forbes as Director in October 1943. Lady Welsh held the post until 1946.

Beauty parlour routine at a Royal Ordnance Factory in November 1943. This particular factory was devoted to the production of shells. The girls in this photograph all worked in the danger area where the shells were actually filled. Following the lessons of the First World War, when a number of munitions workers had been killed by explosions, much stricter regulations were enforced, between 1939 and 1945, for women working in the danger areas of ordnance factories. All abrasive and inflammable substances, including dust and grit, matches, lighters, hair clips, keys, and metal combs, any of which could cause a fatal spark, were kept out of the danger area. Before going into the area, the girls entered a shifting house where they changed into magazine suits of fire-resistant serge, rubber-soled shoes, and fireproof cotton turbans. After a careful wash, the girls applied a special cream to their faces and hands to serve as a mask and to prevent the skin absorbing explosive powders. The 'beauty parlour' had enough tables and mirrors to allow all the girls on a shift to make up in a few minutes.

Girls of the Women's Land Army at work, threshing, on a British farm in December 1942. By the following year, over one-third of all Land Girls were employed in gangs working under the control of the County War Agricultural Executive Committees which supervised the local executive of the government's agricultural policies. For these girls threshing was the main job for eight months of the year. It was dirty, dusty and noisy work which, it was reported, was 'quite ruinous for the complexion'.

Women making parachutes in May 1944. Each
worker has 80 yards of gaily-coloured fabric to
fashion into a parachute. A supply-drop parachute
was made of 140 separate pieces of fabric. Tables 40
ft in length were required when the parachutes were
finally placed in position to be folded.

Mrs Florence Edgar, a former warehouse worker, inspects a Merlin engine at the Rolls-Royce aero engine factory at Hillington, Glasgow, in November 1942. The huge new factory had been planned so that the work could be done mainly by women, and by mid-1943 employed some 20,000 workers, of whom only a small proportion were skilled men.

Women working at a Ministry of Supply steel factory in the north of England, November 1943. They are preparing to shovel waste material spilt from the huge ladle which is filling with 83 tons of molten steel. The women collected the slag in smaller ladles which could be taken away and emptied. At peak, there were over 1,500,000 women employed in the engineering and metal industries, earning an average of £3.10s a week by January 1944.

Overleaf: Women seamen of the British Overseas Airways Corporation moor the Boeing 314A flying-boat *Berwick* in June 1943. Women seamen were employed by B.O.A.C. to work on the fast launches operating in harbour to service the flying-boats which flew on transatlantic routes and to West Africa and Lisbon. The duties of these girls included running and handling the launches, mooring the flying-boats to prevent them swinging round while the engines were being tested, disembarking passengers, scrubbing decks, painting, and splicing ropes. B.O.A.C. had three Boeing 314A Clippers in service during the war.

Previous pages: The A.T.S. dance band in March 1944. All eleven girls were full-time members of the official A.T.S. band; they also played for dances in their spare time. Conducting is Junior Commander Angela Stebbings who joined the A.T.S. as a private in 1939. The idea of forming a band occurred to her in September 1941 even though she had never played an instrument before the war. Beginning with a drum and bugle band, the band eventually became a full military band with brass, woodwind, pipes and drums, comprising nearly fifty musicians. In April 1944 it was organized on the lines of a regular army band and was the only women's military band in Britain at that time. The dance band was formed at the end of 1942.

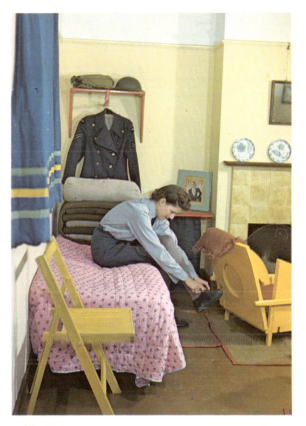

Left: Second Officer Helen Harrison, a woman ferry pilot of the Air Transport Auxiliary, climbing into the cockpit of a Spitfire, November 1943. This auxiliary service was formed in 1939, by a number of experienced pilots who were ineligible for the R.A.F. with the purpose of ferrying aircraft from the factories to R.A.F. aerodromes wherever they were needed. Eight women pilots were admitted to the A.T.A. in 1940. By 1944 there were over 100 women pilots, and the number of women on the ground staff eventually numbered over 900. All the pilots had to have civil flying experience and had to take conversion courses so that they could fly service types. Most of them delivered fighters and twin-engined aircraft although a few delivered four-engined bombers. Between 1939 and 1945 the men and women of the A.T.A. ferried more than 308,000 aircraft.

Right above: The ingenuity of the women of the W.A.A.F. In this bedroom belonging to Flight Officer Stone, a former Civil Air Guard pilot and Nottinghamshire teacher, the shelf and wardrobe fitting and the easy chair were made by W.A.A.F.s of Flying Training Command from scraps of wood rescued from salvage dumps. The photograph was taken in February 1944.

Right below: A member of the Women's Royal Naval Service ('Wrens') demonstrates the art of semaphore on board the submarine depot ship H.M.S. *Forth* on 10 June 1943. The visual signalling course occupied sixteen weeks and the Wrens were expected to be proficient with semaphore flags, signalling projectors, and Aldis lamps. A first-class knowledge of Morse was also required. When the trainees passed out at the end of their course, they had both practical and theoretical experience in signalling. Note the anti-aircraft mounting on the left of the picture.

Members of the Women's Auxiliary Corps (India) drilling in February 1945. Created in April 1942, its members served as clerical workers, cipher, and censorship clerks, storekeepers, radiologists, drivers, mechanics, and caterers. Although Indian society had not yet reached a stage where the average woman would consider joining the W.A.C.(I), recruits were forthcoming, at first mainly from the British and Anglo-Indian communities. Lack of training facilities and poor rates of pay were among the problems which hampered recruiting and expansion, but these difficulties had been largely overcome by July 1945, when the strength of the W.A.C.(I) was 1,178 officers and 10,288 other ranks. The women wearing saris in this picture were permitted not to wear caps.

Previous pages (right): Women of the A.T.S. manning a sound locator in a searchlight battery of Anti-Aircraft Command in January 1943. In September 1941, the Command had been forced to release 30,000 men from searchlight units for the Field Forces. General Sir Frederick Pile, Commander-in-Chief of Anti-Aircraft Command, suggested that women of the A.T.S. and the Home Guard could be used on operational duties, and, despite initial opposition to the idea, the 93rd Mixed Searchlight Regiment went into action in mid-1942. At regimental and battery headquarters level, operations, training and administration still tended to be under male control, but, in the field, all troop officers and most of the personnel were women. The sound locators, which picked up the noise of approaching aircraft, were already obsolete by the time this picture was taken, and had proved inadequate during German night raids in 1940. However, although the *Illustrated* photographer was obviously not permitted to photograph them, searchlight radar sets, known as 'Elsie' sets, were being provided in increasing numbers for searchlight batteries by 1943 and were enabling the searchlights to play a more significant part in the anti-aircraft defence system. The use of A.T.S. and Home Guard personnel enabled Pile to release 71,000 regular gunners during the war. The girls in this picture are wearing special winter clothing.

Previous pages (left): Another view of A.T.S. personnel manning a sound locator at a mixed searchlight battery of Anti-Aircraft Command. Mixed anti-aircraft batteries had been introduced in 1941, about a year before the mixed searchlight units. Although the number of heavy anti-aircraft guns in action in 1945 was virtually the same as at the end of 1940, the use of A.T.S. and Home Guard personnel meant that 60 per cent fewer regular gunners were required. Mixed anti-aircraft units soon achieved standards of drill and turn-out better than most all-male units. Of the A.T.S. searchlight batteries, General Pile wrote: 'The girls lived like men, fought their lights like men, and, alas some of them died like men. Unarmed, they showed great personal bravery...'

Right: Wrens doing physical training exercises on board the submarine depot ship H.M.S. *Forth* in June 1943.

7 THE AFTERMATH

What the human race has failed to learn from history is that war rarely solves anything. Most wars throughout history have merely created an alternative set of circumstances in which the seeds of future conflict have been sown. The defeat of France in the Franco-Prussian War of 1870-71, and the unification of Germany which accompanied it, brought Germany into a dominant position in Europe and helped to create the opposing alliance systems which polarized around these two nations and led Europe into the most horrifying war she had ever known. Following the First World War, the Versailles Settlement, coupled with the moral exhaustion of the belligerent powers, created the Europe of Hitler and led to the second global conflict within twenty-five years.

Even after the quarter of a century which has elapsed since the end of the Second World War, it is still impossible to measure its full effects. Rivalries between individual nations have been replaced by rivalries between opposing ideologies and massive power blocs. The establishment of Soviet influence over the whole of eastern Europe substituted one set of armed camps for another. During the war, the United States and Russia took the centre of the world stage and have occupied that position ever since. The new ideological rivalries forced these leading powers to speed up post-war reconstruction in the interests of their own security and that of their allies or satellites. In some cases those allies were yesterday's enemies. Thus, ironically, the defeated nations have prospered as much, if not more, than some of the victors of 1945. West Germany and Japan, prostrate and devastated at the end of the war, are once again among the world's leading industrial nations.

The power of Britain and France was to some extent already beginning to decline by 1914 and was further weakened by their massive sacrifices in the First World War. The Second World War merely served to hasten this process. Certainly the pattern of British society changed during the 1939-1945 period, although some of the trends were beginning to appear during the earlier struggle. Both crises had inevitably led to an increase in the size and power of the machinery of state; in organizing a nation for total war, the government had been forced to spread its net further and further into the daily lives of the people. When the war ended, both the machinery and the power remained. The change in the class structure had really come during the First World War and there was a less evident shift in the balance between the classes from 1939 to 1945. However, if society remained substantially the same as it had been in the inter-war years, there was a greater levelling of standards. Taxation, rationing, higher wages, the sharing of common dangers, and the Beveridge Report of 1942, which helped pave the way for the post-war Welfare State, all played their part in this. The war increased the determination of British men and women to press for greater security, decent wages and living standards and some taste of consumer luxuries. Meanwhile, as in every war, the technological spin-off had benefits for peacetime. Light industry had expanded considerably, making people less dependent on the old heavy industries for employment. To ensure that the materials of war were produced, the government and employers had to court and cajole their employees to an unprecedented degree. This gave the working classes a wider political, social and economic power base than ever before and brought the mass consumer society much nearer. The National Health Service kept them healthier, radio and television made them better informed and the availability of cars for more and more people made them increasingly mobile. If one issue was paramount in 1945 it was that of housing. The photographs in this section reflect not only the devastation which the war had brought but also something of the movement towards a resumption of normality. In Britain, the government had estimated during the war that three-quarters of a million new homes would be needed after it was all over. To meet immediate post-war requirements, an emergency programme was instituted involving, among other measures, the construction of prefabricated houses. The 'pre-fab' shown here illustrates the type of temporary home which it was hoped to provide for many of those who had been 'bombed-out'. Yet few things reflect the extent to which promises could not be kept as well as the story of the prefabricated homes. Few families ever actually got to live in the steel pre-fab as shown in the following pages. Shortages of pressed steel led to a modification of the original programme and to the use of less satisfactory materials such as wood and asbestos cement. The fact that some of these temporary dwellings can still be seen, and are still lived in, is a corrective to the assumption that post-war reconstruction has been completed. These, at one end of the scale, and the Berlin Wall at the other, testify to the tasks which remain ahead.

The ruins of the Norman town of Caen in 1945, one year after the battle in Normandy which followed D-Day. Caen, an important road and rail centre on the eastern flank of the Normandy beach-head, formed the hinge of German communications in Normandy and became one of the decisive points in the battle. Originally scheduled for capture by the evening of D-Day, it was defended bitterly by the German armoured divisions and was not liberated until 9 July, when the Canadians entered the town. A sad monument to the war, it suffered great destruction in June and July 1944 when over two-thirds of its buildings were reduced to rubble or heavily damaged. Life was just beginning to return to Caen in 1945 and German prisoners were still in the streets, helping to clear the wreckage. The historic town on the banks of the Orne, which has strong links with William the Conqueror, showed the scars of war for many years and it was 1959 before rebuilding was completed.

An informal photograph of Hitler, probably
taken at the Teehaus, a small pavilion near the
Berghof at Obersalzburg, where Hitler would
sometimes go for meals, or coffee and cakes, with
members of his initimate circle at his Bavarian
retreat. Often he would doze off in one of the
comfortable armchairs. As the war progressed and
Germany's position deteriorated, such moments of
relaxation became increasingly rare. Finally, with the
Red Army fighting in the streets of Berlin and closing
in on the Führerbunker beneath the Reich
Chancellery, Hitler shot himself on 30 April 1945.
His 'Thousand-Year Reich' had lasted little over a
decade.

Eva Braun, photographed at the Berghof,
Obersalzburg, known to Hitler's intimate circle as
the 'Grand Hotel'. Eva Braun shared the last
moments of Hitler's life as his wife, having
married him in the Führerbunker on 28 April 1945,
just before midnight, and less than forty-eight hours
before his death. She had first met Hitler in October
1929 when she was working in Heinrich Hoffmann's
photographic shop in Munich. After Geli Raubal's
suicide in 1931, Eva Braun gradually began to
replace her in Hitler's affections. Although she may
have become Hitler's mistress as early as 1932, she
often suffered from loneliness and unhappiness,
caused by Hitler's frequent absences and increasing
involvement in national politics. A gay and simple
girl, she was at first more interested in films and
novels than in the Nazi movement, and never actually
became a Party member. It is doubtful whether
Hitler's feelings for her ever extended as far as love,
but after her two unsuccessful suicide attempts in
1932 and 1935, he undoubtedly felt a moral
obligation to her and was flattered by her loyalty and
devotion. Thus, in 1936, he installed her as mistress
of the enlarged Berghof, where she was to spend
some two-thirds of her time between 1936 and 1945.
Their relationship was always a shadowy one, Hitler
being reluctant to recognize officially an affair which
might have detracted from his highly moral image as
Führer. To questions about marriage, Hitler always
replied: 'I am already married to Germany'.
Eva Braun invariably had to disappear to her rooms
whenever important visitors came to the Berghof.
As she grew older she became a mature, elegant and
self-possessed woman and a fierce but blind partisan
of Nazi domination. Although she referred to herself
as 'Miss No Private Life' (following a speech by
Goebbels in which he declared that the Führer was
totally devoted to Germany and had no private life)
she eventually began to emerge from obscurity,
finally coming briefly on to the centre of the stage of
history during those last hours in the Führerbunker.
Shortly before their marriage, Hitler declared: 'I
have now decided, at the end of my life's journey, to
marry the young girl who, after years of faithful
friendship, freely chose to share my fate in a city
already almost completely besieged'. Eva Hitler, as
she now was, committed suicide by taking poison
on 30 April, her body being burnt in the Chancellery
garden, although it was never positively identified.

Previous pages: A ruined symbol of the Third
Reich – the Reich Chancellery in Berlin. Hitler had
described the previous Chancellery as 'fit for a soap
company' when he moved into it in 1933. In
January 1938, Albert Speer, Hitler's architect and
Inspector General of Buildings, was summoned by
Hitler and asked if he could design and build a new
Chancellery for him on the Voss Strasse by 10
January 1939, less than a year away. Speer promised
that he could. Almost immediately, buildings on the
Voss Strasse were razed to make way for the new
building. Speer rejected any complex plan in view of
the time factor, but had to order many components
and decide on colours and designs of fittings even
before he had settled architectural details, mainly
because of delivery problems on such items as
hand-made rugs. The oblong site led him to design
a succession of rooms on a long axis. After visitors
had arrived in a court of honour, they would be
taken to a reception room from which 17 ft-high
double doors opened out into a large mosaic-clad hall.
Then, ascending several steps, they would pass
through a round room with a domed ceiling into a
gallery 480 ft long with deep window niches to
filter the light. Finally came Hitler's reception hall.
Hitler was delighted with the plans and with the
design of his study, which had gilded panels over the
doors depicting the Virtues – Wisdom, Prudence,
Fortitude and Justice. He interfered little in the work
which, apart from those all over Germany who were
producing components, occupied 4,500 workers
toiling in two shifts to meet the deadline. Hitler was
particularly pleased with the long tramp from the
entrance for guests and diplomats to the reception
hall, and was not worried about the polished marble
floors: 'Diplomats should have practice in moving
on a slippery surface' was his reply when asked.
The new Chancellery was finished forty-eight hours
ahead of schedule and, when addressing the work
force, Hitler spoke of the structure '. . . that will
outlast the centuries. . . This is the first architectural
creation of the new, great German Reich'. Little over
six years later, already badly damaged by British
and American air raids, it was further reduced to
rubble by Soviet artillery in the Battle of Berlin.

Her Majesty Queen Elizabeth (now the Queen
Mother) talks to Allied soldiers and airmen at a
Buckingham Palace garden party for repatriated
prisoners of war in June 1945. Some 1,100
servicemen from Britain and the Commonwealth
were present on this occasion.

Leonard Hickman (who later became Features Editor of the *Sun* newspaper), then a twenty-eight-year old ex-serviceman, with his wife Florence and children Pamela (five) and John (three and a half) inspect a prefabricated house in May 1944. Two months earlier, Churchill had announced that the government was already preparing the construction of 500,000 'prefabs' to help solve the housing problems caused by war damage. Their manufacture, he said, 'would be treated as a military evolution handled by the government, with private industry harnessed to its service'.

Opposite: Leonard Hickman and his family inspect the interior of one of the new prefabricated houses and are seen here examining the compact wardrobe and cupboard fittings in the bedroom. The emergency scheme announced by Churchill in March 1944 resulted, after the war, in no more than 160,000 utilitarian 'prefabs'. Although they were never intended as anything more than a temporary solution, some of these houses are still being lived in today.

Overleaf: Soldiers and girls pose for the photographer in a Universal Carrier at Butlin's Holiday Camp at Filey in August 1945. *Illustrated* reported that holidays in 1945 were filled with drawbacks, including overcrowding, profiteering, insufficient accommodation or amusements, and greatly increased costs. From an 'all-found' price of 45s a week before the war, the cost of a holiday had gone up to £5.5s at most boarding houses. Petrol rationing and the deterioration of railway stock even made travel to resorts difficult, while luxuries such as buckets and spades were treasured heirlooms from pre-war days. In this situation, the holiday camps seemed to offer the best chance of a good holiday. W. E. 'Billy' Butlin had started his first camp at Skegness in the mid-1930s. Filey had been still on the drawing boards in 1939, but had been completed for use by the R.A.F. When the war ended, the government had to decide whether to cling to more than 100 requisitioned holiday camps at a time when war workers and ex-servicemen were expecting their first real holiday for years. Part of Filey had been handed back and within four weeks was ready to receive holidaymakers. When this picture was taken the visitors were separated from the airmen by a barbed-wire fence, while Royal Engineers were using the Carrier to drag beach obstacles away. An 'all-found' holiday at Butlins in 1945 cost between £5.10s and £6.10s a week. Butlin (later Sir William Butlin) had four other camps, at Clacton, Ayr, Skegness and Pwllheli, none of which had yet been de-requisitioned. Such camps became a holiday fashion in the post-war era, and millions now take this form of holiday every year.